Nini Le was born into poverty on August 28, 1981, after the Vietnam War. She, her mother and siblings tried to escape Vietnam twenty-two times, risking their lives in search for a better future and freedom. Because of their strong determination, courage, and perseverance they've eventually succeeded and arrived in America on her eighth birthday and re-united with her father. She began to learn the language, studied hard, and graduated at the top of her class. She had a full scholarship to the University of Connecticut and graduated in 2004. She moved to California after college and bought her first home at 26 years old and thus, achieving the 'American dream.'

NINI LE

TEARS OF JOY

Austin Macauley Publishers
LONDON * CAMBRIDGE * NEW YORK * SHARJAH

Copyright © Nini Le 2024

All rights reserved. No part of this publication may be reproduced, distributed, or transmitted in any form or by any means, including photocopying, recording, or other electronic or mechanical methods, without the prior written permission of the publisher, except in the case of brief quotations embodied in critical reviews and certain other non-commercial uses permitted by copyright law. For permission requests, write to the publisher.

Any person who commits any unauthorized act in relation to this publication may be liable to criminal prosecution and civil claims for damages.

Ordering Information

Quantity sales: Special discounts are available on quantity purchases by corporations, associations, and others. For details, contact the publisher at the address below.

Publisher's Cataloging-in-Publication data

Le, Nini

Tears Of Joy

ISBN 9781649791122 (Paperback)

ISBN 9781649791139 (ePub e-book)

Library of Congress Control Number: 2024911702

www.austinmacauley.com/us

First Published 2024

Austin Macauley Publishers LLC

40 Wall Street, 33rd Floor, Suite 3302

New York, NY 10005

USA

mail-usa@austinmacauley.com

+1 (646) 5125767

I dedicate this book to my mother, who inspired me to write this book and to share my story.

Without my mother and her strength and courage, I would not be where I am today.

I would like to acknowledge Austin Macauley Publishers for believing in me and helping me publish this book. Thank you for letting me share a piece of my history.

I was born on August 28, 1981 in a small town in southern Vietnam. My parents, older sister, older brother, and I lived on a farm. Our house, though small, was very warm and cozy. We lived on a plain next to the "Cuu Long" (Nine Dragon) River. It was my father's hometown, where most of Vietnam's crops were produced. Almost everyone who lived here were farmers, each with their own farm and rice field.

The land was extremely peaceful. There were many crooked rivers, which brought rich soil to the crops and enriched the coconut fields. There were also a great number of other fruitful trees that brought forward delicious fruits all year round. Some of these were mangoes, bananas, and guavas; each branch was weighted with beautiful fruits, especially under the warm summer sun.

All the children here had to help their parents at home and in the field. The older ones had to help tend the fields, breed the bulls, and feed the chickens and pigs. Not many children were able to go to school. Those who were able to were very lucky.

Before 1975, my country was divided in two. The Communists were in the North, and the Republicans were in the South. My father was a naval officer in the army of the Vietnamese Republicans.

On April 30, 1975, "Viet Cong" (Vietnamese Communists) took over South Vietnam. They forced all of the Republican officers and workers to go to the "re-educational camps". At these camps, my father and those who worked for the previous government had to work very hard in the woods, under the control of the Communists.

After three years, my father was released from the camp. He went back to his hometown and was not allowed to leave town without the government's permission. Since he was a Republican officer, my father could not find any decent job. He had to work on the farm to earn a living.

My mother was a teacher in high school. In 1980, she moved back to my father's hometown and took a teaching job there. I was born here in a small temple, which the "Viet Cong" turned into a hospital. Most of the people lost their freedom. People could not go to church because the "Viet Cong" turned the churches into granaries.

Every day when my mother was at school, my father stayed home to take care of my sister, brother, and me. Once she came home, my father went out to the field to work.

My father was very devoted to his family. He worked hard to try to support us. My father plowed and tended the rice field every day. Sometimes my sister and brother tried to help him, but I was too little to do anything.

Every day was the same. When my father came home from his hard work, my mother brought out the food, and we all got together to eat dinner. Time went by very fast. These were some of the happiest moments for us. Yet, life began to change drastically.

Under the watchful eyes of the governor and his followers, my father had no freedom. Once in a while, my father was forced to work with others who were in similar situations, to build dams and rebuild the dirt roads. The work was very difficult. As a result, in February 1982, he escaped from his hometown to Saigon City. Here, he lived illegally in his parents-in-laws' apartment.

My mother continued her teaching and tried her best to take care of us. Life was very hard and meaningless without my father. All that time, I was only eight months old. My mother told me that every afternoon, when the sun began to fade, I always looked out into the horizon and across the river, as if waiting for his return. Nevertheless, every day was the same, my father never returned.

In May 1983, my mother decided to go to Saigon City to reunite with my father. We left our house, our field, our farm, and everything we had behind and moved to Saigon. In Saigon, my aunts, uncles, parents, sister, brother, and I lived with my grandparents in their small apartment.

My grandparents' apartment was near the market. The streets were always crowded with people from early morning to late afternoon. The local market was a very colorful and noisy place, crowded with interesting people and many things to see. People could even have their shoes shined or get their fortunes told at the market.

In my grandparents' apartment, I spoke the first word and walked the first step. When I was four, I went to a kindergarten school near my house. Every afternoon, my mother came to school to take me home. My teacher told my mother how talented I was at coloring and drawing.

Once in a while, my mother took us to the marketplace on Main Street. We were overjoyed because the market was a crowded place filled with tall buildings and vehicles such as motorcycles, bicycles, and tricycles. Life was much better here than in my father's hometown.

Every year during "Tet" (Vietnamese New Year), my grandmother made many kinds of food: cakes, candies, and dried fruits. My aunts bought "hoa mai", yellow flowers that represent luck and happiness, and put them on the tables and on top of the drawer in the living room, where our ancestors were worshipped. Whenever we saw these yellow flowers, watermelons, and firecrackers, we knew that "Tet" was nearby. That meant we were able to get new clothes.

Because my mother's salary as a teacher could not help our family to survive, we had to depend greatly on my grandparents, aunts, and uncles financially. My father could not find anything to do to help us, so he decided to escape from Vietnam to find a better life for us.

From 1983 to 1985, my father attempted to escape numerous times but without success. Although the government couldn't catch him, he always came home wounded. He was injured trying to crawl through wired fences so he wouldn't get caught. Despite all of the hardships he had to face, my father refused to give up the attempt at finding a new life in America—a better life, a life of freedom and prosperity.

In July 1985, my father escaped from Vietnam on a sailboat with six other people. The escape was very dangerous because they were caught in a storm. They were stuck in the middle of the ocean for approximately two weeks. In these two weeks, they had to face starvation and sickness. But finally, they were able to arrive successfully in the Philippines with the help of God.

My father stayed in the refugee camp in Palawan for a year. He came to America in 1986, and he has lived in Connecticut ever since. My father began a new life by learning the language and working at a nearby factory. My father worked very hard so he could have enough money to send back to his family.

In 1987, I was in first grade, my sister was in seventh, and my brother was in third. Our school was very small but lovable. It had a large iron gate in front of the school, which opened to welcome us students every single morning. There were rows of bright, gorgeous red flowering trees that surrounded our school.

Because of our eagerness to be united with my father, my mother took my sister, brother, and me on many escapes. We attempted to escape twenty-two times and were caught by the Vietnamese Communists three times.

Once we got caught, the "Viet Cong" tied all of our hands together with a rope. My hands were not tied together because I was too little. They forced us to go into the truck, which was crowded with prisoners. Then they took us to jail. We were put in four different jails. The jails were small but packed with many people, which consisted of killers, thieves, and people who tried to escape like us. The jail was dark, where no sunlight could be seen and no fresh air could escape through.

Our escapes were full of hardships and dangers. During one of our escapes, the leader of our group hid us in the bushes of wild plants. We stayed there, waiting for the night to fall so our boat would come to take us to the sea. In those bushes, the ants and bees attacked us and stung our bodies, and yet we didn't dare move. We had to bear the pain because we were afraid of getting caught.

One time, we hid in a place dense with wild bushes, and two fishermen saw us. They told each other that they would report us to the police. When they left, we were very afraid. We rushed into the nearby wood of dates, which were full of thorny branches. Our escape failed that time. When we got home, my grandmother had to spend many hours trying to take the thorns out of our fragile bodies using a sharp needle.

On a horrible dark night, we were on a small boat, leading us to the escaping one. The river was very quiet. Suddenly, another boat appeared with pirates holding long swords. They stopped us and forced our boat to turn into a small tunnel that was filled with watergrass. Then, they took all our belongings. After that, they let us go. We returned home and were caught on the way.

On October 7, 1988, we escaped again after we were released from jail the night before. After my father received the news about our escape, he was very worried because there was a big storm at the time. He didn't eat or sleep. Every night, he prayed to God and Mary for our safety and that someday we would be united.

Our boat was in the middle of the ocean when the storm came. There were 73 of us on the boat, trying to survive and fighting desperately against death. We were surrounded by water and total darkness. Many times, the powerful wind and waves knocked against our little boat, trying to sink us to the bottom of the lifeless ocean. We thought we were all going to die, so we prayed and waited for our deaths. But the boat moved slowly forward.

We all laid motionless on the damp floor of the boat. Only a few men had the strength to control the boat. My mother used all of her remaining strength to try to keep us alive. She never stopped praying to God. Our lives and destiny were relied only in the powerful hands of God.

After three days and three nights of fighting and struggling against the storm, starvation, and thirst, we managed to survive. Our boat was almost sinking, and we were face-to-face with death when, suddenly, an Australian oil freighter appeared out of nowhere. It was as if God had been deeply touched by our bravery, so he opened up his hands to save us.

They let down the rope, and all of us climbed into the oil freighter. All of us were extremely weak and weary, and some of us could not even walk. They gave us food to eat and water to drink, and we were taken care of by the Australian doctors who were on the ship. We stayed on the ship for one night, and then the next day they brought us to Pulau Bidong.

Pulau Bidong Island belongs to Malaysia. It stood alone and was surrounded by nothing but water. The island had many coconut trees and mountains with beautiful wild plants and flowers. There was a spring running from the top of the mountain down to the valley. About 12,000 Vietnamese refugees resided on this island at that time, waiting to be immigrated.

We stayed on the island for about 10 months. My sister, brother, and I attended school to learn English. We learned how to say words such as "dog", "cat", and "my name is". My mother worked voluntarily to help other refugees who were on the island.

On August 25, 1989, we left the refugee camp to go to the United States. We stayed in Hong Kong for three days and arrived at Bradley International Airport on August 28, 1989, right on my eighth birthday. My father and some of his friends waited for us at the airport. When we saw my father, we all hugged each other as joyful tears rolled down our cheeks. It was a happy moment for our family as we reunited with my father. These tears were indeed the tears of joy.

My father brought us to our small apartment in Hartford, Connecticut. Three days later, my sister, brother, and I had to go to school. At first, I couldn't understand or learn anything because my English was so limited. I was very sad, frustrated, and disappointed. With the help and encouragement of my parents and teachers, I did not give up and worked very hard. Little by little, I was able to catch up with my classmates. I received several awards for writing and art, which gave me a lot of joy, pride, and self-esteem.

On August 28, 1993, on my 12th birthday, our family moved to Windsor, Connecticut. Our house was very big, with a garden filled with flowers and fruit trees. Our life began to change in our new house. I often remembered and missed the small apartment back in Vietnam where we used to live. Every time I thought back to my early childhood and all the happy and painful moments I've had, tears rolled down my eyes. My new life in America was definitely hard. Nevertheless, I continued to live and work hard so that I could be somebody someday.